Editor
Eric Migliaccio

Managing Editor
Ina Massler Levin, M.A.

Illustrator
Alexandra Artigas

Cover Artist
Denise Bauer

Art Production Manager
Kevin Barnes

Imaging
James Edward Grace

Publisher
Mary D. Smith, M.S. Ed.

Teacher Created Resources
TCR 3914

Indoor & Outdoor Games

Going Beyond Duck, Duck, Goose

Grades K–6

Author

Cary Pyle

Teacher
Created
Resources

Teacher Created Resources, Inc.

6421 Industry Way

Westmin

www.teac

ISBN: 97

D1501583

©2005 Teacher (

Reprinted, 2013

Made in U.S.A.

The classroom teacher may reproduce the materi~~ls in this book and/or CD for use in a single~~
classroom only. The reproduction of any part of
entire school or school system is strictly prohibit
recorded in any form without written permission
material, which may be stored on the purchaser's

Table of Contents

Introduction

Indoor and Outdoor Games: Going Beyond Duck, Duck, Goose was written because children enjoy playing games time and time again. Many teachers realize the importance of offering practical games that require minimal preparation and equipment. These two factors were given careful consideration in designing this book, and each game has been successfully played (not to mention enjoyed!) by groups of elementary-school children.

Indoor and Outdoor Games: Going Beyond Duck, Duck, Goose provides a variety of both indoor and outdoor games that elementary-school teachers, recreation leaders, and other individuals working with young people can use. These games are not a substitute for a physical-education curriculum, but rather a resource for entertainment.

The games are organized by age range and subdivided depending on whether they are most appropriate for indoor and outdoor enjoyment. The age range is merely a suggestion, and you can adjust the games accordingly. After all, no one has more of an understanding of your group of children and their needs than you do.

These games will become favorites for you and your group of children as you challenge yourself to go beyond Duck, Duck, Goose.

Note: see page 48 for a complete listing of the individual games contained in this book.

Beanbag Toss

Equipment

* beanbags

* different-sized containers

* masking tape

Set-Up

Place a strip of masking tape on the floor to define each of the four lines behind which players must toss the beanbags. The players line up behind the four lines. Empty containers are placed side-by-side an adequate distance from the four lines. Each container is given a point value according to its size (smallest container has highest point value).

Directions

The first player in line takes the beanbags and tries to throw them in any of the containers. Then he or she picks up the beanbags and gives them to the next player in line. If a player steps beyond the foul line, no points are awarded. After a players turn, his or her points are tallied and recorded. The player who scores the most points wins.

Variation

Use different-colored beanbags. Write down the color of each beanbag on slips of paper and place them in a container. Before each player's turn, secretly select a slip of paper. After the player throws the beanbags, reveal the mystery color. If the player threw the mystery color beanbag into a container, the point value of the container is doubled.

Dog and Bone

Equipment

* chair

* small object (e.g., chalkboard eraser)

Set-Up

Choose a player to be the dog and have that player sit in a chair in front of the room with his or her back to the other players. The bone (i.e., the small object) is on the floor under his or her chair. The other players remain seated on the floor.

Directions

Point to a player to walk up and try to grab the bone. If the dog hears that player coming, he or she says, "Arf, arf," and he or she remains the dog; if not, the player who successfully retrieves the bone becomes the new dog.

Follow the Leader

Equipment

✳ no equipment required

Set-Up

The group sits on the floor, forming a circle. Choose a player to be "It" and have him or her leave the room. After "It" leaves the room, point to a player to be the leader.

Directions

To begin play, the leader begins a motion (e.g., clapping hands, snapping fingers, nodding head) that the other players mimic. When "It" returns to the room, he or she stands in the center of the circle. The leader changes motions periodically. "It" gets three guesses as to who is changing the motion. If "It" guesses correctly, he or she remains "It"; if not, the leader becomes the new "It." The players should attempt to confuse "It" by looking at each other as they follow the leader.

Four Corners

Equipment

* ✳ blindfold

* ✳ chair

Set-Up

The group sits on the floor. Position a chair in the center of the room, equidistant from each corner. Number the corners of the room 1, 2, 3, and 4. Choose a player to be "It" and have him or her sit in the chair wearing a blindfold.

Directions

On the signal to begin, the other players walk quietly to a corner. When everyone is standing in a corner, "It" calls out a number. Any player standing in that corner is eliminated. The game continues in the same manner until one player remains. Then he or she becomes the new "It."

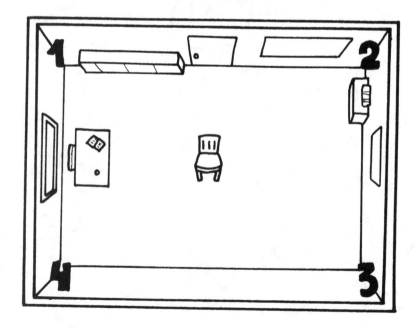

Fruit Basket

Equipment

✴ small, soft, differently-colored balls

Set-Up

The group sits on the floor, forming a circle. Give the balls to the players spaced evenly around the circle. The colored balls are imaginary fruit (e.g., the red ball is an apple).

Directions

On the signal to begin, the players holding the fruit pass it quickly to the players to their left, keeping the fruit moving at all times. When a player holds two pieces of fruit at once, he or she is eliminated. As the number of players dwindle, some pieces of fruit are removed. The game continues in the same manner until two players remain.

Variation

Call "reverse" for some unpredictability to the game.

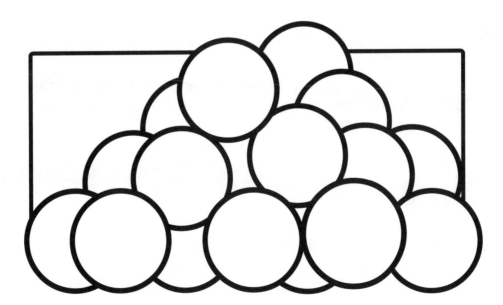

It's a Toss-Up

Equipment

* assorted colored balloons

* watch or clock

Set-Up

Divide the group into equal teams of four to five players. Each team sits on the floor, forming circles in separate areas of the room. Each team receives a differently-colored balloon.

Directions

Set a time limit. On the signal to begin, each team tosses their balloon in the air and tries to keep it up. The players must stay seated and take turns tapping the balloon. When the time limit expires, the teams whose balloon did not touch the ground receive a point. The game ends after a predetermined number of rounds or after a designated point total is reached. The team that scores the most points wins.

Variations

Write down the color of each team's balloon on slips of paper and place them in a container. Before each round, secretly select a slip of paper. At the end of the round, reveal the mystery color. If the team whose color was chosen did not allow their balloon to touch the ground, they receive a bonus point!

Jump the River

Equipment

✳ yarn

Set-Up

Stretch two pieces of yarn a short distance apart across the play area to represent the river. The players line up facing the river.

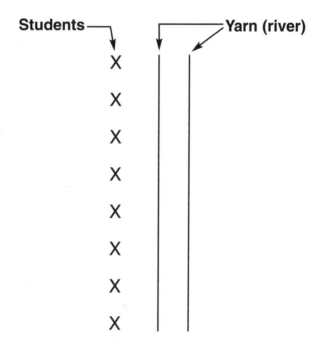

Directions

To begin play, the first player in line runs and tries to jump over the river. If he or she is successful, he or she goes to the end of the line; if not and his or her feet "get wet," he or she is eliminated. After everyone has one try, make the river wider. Play continues in the same manner until one player remains.

Mum's the Word

Equipment

✳ small object (e.g., thimble)

Set-Up

Divide the group into equal teams of five to six players seated at a table.

Directions

Show all the players the object you will hide and then have everyone place their heads on their tables so they cannot see while the object is hidden in plain sight. Set a time limit. On the signal to begin, the players walk around the room searching for the hidden object. When they find it, they quietly return to their tables without revealing the location of the object. Anyone giving away the whereabouts of the object disqualifies his or her team. The first team that has all its players find the object—or the team with the most players knowing the whereabouts of the object when the time limit expires—wins. In order to insure credibility, have the players whisper to you the location of the hidden object.

Police Officer

Equipment

✳ no equipment required (see Variations)

Set-Up

Choose two players to be police officers. The other players remain seated at tables. Both police officers try to memorize where each player is sitting. After taking a few moments to closely observe the room, they leave the room.

Directions

When the police officers leave the room, the other players must change places with someone. After everyone changes places, the police officers return to the room and attempt to return each player to their original chair while the other players silently watch. Set a time limit. When the time limit expires, count the number of players sitting in their original chair. The duo that correctly puts the most players back in their original chairs are declared "Chiefs of Police." Before beginning a new round, everyone must return to his or her original chair.

Variations

Before playing this game, have students use construction paper, scissors, and markers to make their own police badges.

Silent Ball

Equipment

* jelly ball

Set-Up

The group stands on the floor, scattered around the play area.

Directions

Decide who will begin. On the signal to begin, the player holding the ball throws it to another player.

The players are eliminated if they do any of the following:

* drop the ball
* make a bad toss

* throw to the same player who threw to them
* talk during the game

Once a player is eliminated, he or she sits down. The game continues in the same manner until one player remains standing.

Blob

Equipment

✳ four traffic cones

Set-Up

Place a traffic cone in each corner of the play area to establish boundaries. Choose two players to be the Blob and have them join hands. The other players scatter inside the play area.

Directions

On the signal to begin, the Blob chases and attempts to tag the other players with their free hands. When a player is tagged, he or she joins hands with the Blob and helps tag another player. When another player is tagged, a new Blob is formed (two Blobs of two players). Anyone who runs outside the boundaries also becomes part of the Blob. No tag counts if a Blob separates. The game continues in the same manner until only two players remain. They become the new Blob.

Circle Soccer

Equipment

✳ soccer ball

Set-Up

The players form a large circle. Divide the group into two equal teams. Each team occupies half of the circle.

Directions

Decide who will begin; that team starts with the soccer ball. To begin play, the team that has the soccer ball attempts to kick the ball across the opponent's half of the circle. The players may use only their feet to deflect the ball. When a team kicks the ball across the opponent's half of the circle, they score a goal. A goal is not scored if the ball is kicked over the heads of the players. If the ball stops rolling inside the circle, kick the ball to the team that the ball was rolling towards. The team that scores the most goals wins.

14

Hoopla

Equipment

* several beanbags

* four hula hoops

Set-Up

Place a hula hoop in each corner of the play area. Place the same number of beanbags in each hoop. Divide the group into four equal teams. Have each team stand near a hoop. This is their home base.

Directions

Set a time limit. On the signal to begin, each team takes beanbags from other hula hoops and puts them in theirs. Each player may take only one beanbag at a time and must put it inside the hula hoop before getting another one. When the time limit expires, the team with the most beanbags in their hoop wins that particular round. The game continues in the same manner until a designated point total is reached.

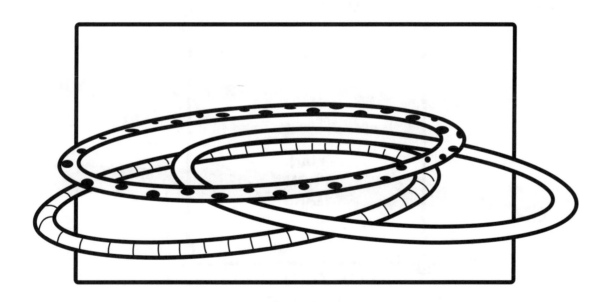

Man from Mars

Equipment

✳ four traffic cones

Set-Up

Place a traffic cone in each corner of the play area to establish boundaries. Choose a player to be the "Man from Mars" and have that player stand in the center of the play area. The remaining players are the "Earthlings" and stand at a safety zone located at each end of the play area.

Directions

To being play, the Earthlings call, "Man from Mars, will you take us to the stars?" The Man from Mars replies, "Only if you are wearing the color_____." The players wearing that color attempt to run to the other side without getting tagged. Those tagged join the Man from Mars in the center of the play area. Anyone who runs outside the boundaries also joins the Man from Mars. Play continues in the same manner until one player remains. Then he or she becomes the new Man from Mars.

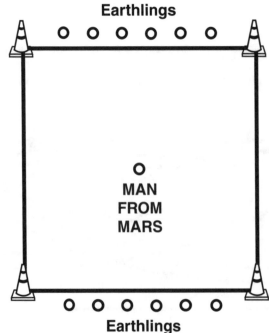

Mousetrap

Equipment

✳ no equipment required

Set-Up

Divide the group into two unequal groups. The larger group, the mousetrap, forms a circle with hands joined, facing center. The smaller group, the mice, are outside the circle.

Directions

Three signals are announced during the game:

✳ On the first signal, "Happy play," the mice play happily outside the circle.

✳ On the second signal, "Bridges up," the mousetrap is opened (circle players raise their joined hands to form arches) and the mice run in and out of it. The mice cannot run in and out of the mousetrap through adjacent openings.

✳ On the third signal, "Bridges down," the mousetrap is closed (circle players lower their hands). Any mice caught in the mousetrap join the circle to make the mousetrap.

The game continues in the same manner until all the mice are caught. The players take turns being the mousetrap and mice.

Old Witch

Equipment

✳ four traffic cones

Set-Up

Place a traffic cone in each corner of the play area to establish boundaries. Choose a player to be the Old Witch. The other players stand at a safety zone located at each end of the play area.

Directions

To begin play, the players call out, "Old Witch, Old Witch, what time is it?" The Old Witch replies, "It is _____ o'clock." The players take that many steps forward. Play continues in the same manner until the Old Witch replies, "It is midnight!" Then the players attempt to run to the other side without getting tagged. Those tagged join the Old Witch in the center of the play area. Anyone who runs outside the boundaries also joins the Old Witch. Play continues in the same manner until just one player remains. Then he or she becomes the new Old Witch.

Variation

Choose a player to be the Old Leprechaun, Pilgrim, Elf, etc., according to a holiday.

Rescue Relay

Equipment

* ✳ four traffic cones

Set-Up

Place a traffic cone in each corner of the play area, forming a narrow rectangle. Divide the group into two equal teams. Choose a rescuer for each team. Each team forms a line behind a cone at the finish line. The rescuer from each team stands behind a cone at the start line, facing his or her team.

Directions

On the signal to begin, the rescuers run forward and grasp the outstretched hand of the first player in line. Together, the rescuer and the player run back to the finish line. The original rescuers remain at the start line, and the first players run back and rescue the second players in line. Then the first player stays and the second players run back and get the third players in line, and so on. The relay continues in the same manner until all the players are rescued. The team that rescues all of its players first wins.

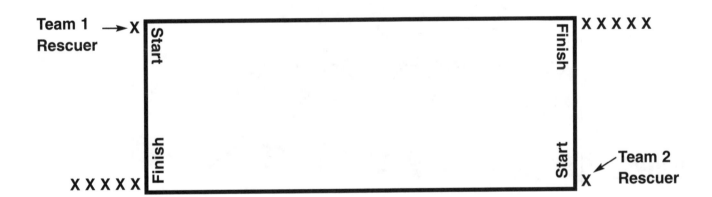

Runaway Caboose

Equipment

✳ no equipment required

Set-Up

Choose a player to be the runaway caboose. Divide the other players into trains of three. Each player is a boxcar and places his or her hands on the waist of the player in front. The first player in a train is the engine.

Directions

On the signal to begin, the trains chug around the play area trying to dodge the runaway caboose and not allowing it to hook on. When the runaway caboose connects to a train, the engine of that train detaches and becomes the new runaway caboose.

S-C-A-T

Equipment

✳ playground ball

Set-Up

The players form a circle. Assign each player a number.

Directions

Decide who will begin. The person who has the ball stands in the center of the circle, throws the ball up in the air, and calls out a number. Everyone scatters except the player whose number was called. That player immediately retrieves the ball and yells, "Scat!" When the other players hear this, they must stop at once and not move. The person who retrieves the ball may take three steps in any direction. Then he and she rolls the ball in an attempt to hit another player. If hit, that player gets a letter (S, C, A, or T); if not, the roller gets a letter. The player whose number was called throws the ball in the air next. Anyone who gets the four letters S-C-A-T is eliminated.

Squirrel in the Trees

Equipment

❉ no equipment required

Set-Up

Several pairs of players form trees by facing each other and putting their hands on each other's shoulders. The other players are squirrels and stand inside each tree. Choose a player to be an extra squirrel and stand outside the trees.

Directions

On the signal to begin, all the squirrels move to another tree, and the extra squirrel attempts to find an unoccupied tree. Only one squirrel is allowed in a tree. After each squirrel moves into a tree, he or she can change places with a player forming the tree so that all the players are eventually active.

Steal the Bacon

Equipment

✳ handkerchief or towel

Set-Up

Divide the group into two equal teams, forming two lines facing each other. The players on each team number off so that the players with identical numbers are sitting opposite from each other. The bacon (a handkerchief or towel) is placed in the center at a point equidistant from both teams.

Directions

To begin play, call out a number. The player on each team having that number rushes to the center and attempts to snatch the bacon and return it to his or her side without being tagged. If a player successfully returns it to his or her side without being tagged, he or she scores a point for his or her team; if not, no point is scored. If a player on the other team tags him or her, then that player's team gets a point. The team that scores the most points wins.

Variation

Call out players' names if the group cannot be divided into two equal teams.

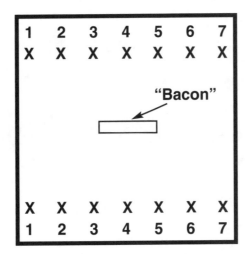

Balloon Volleyball

Equipment

* balloon

* two chairs

* masking tape

* yarn

Set-Up

Mark the boundaries with masking tape. Stretch the net (piece of yarn) between two chairs across the center of the play area. Divide the group into two equal teams. Teams space themselves and sit facing each other on opposite sides of the net.

Directions

Decide which team will serve. On the signal to begin, the balloon is served into play. The players must stay seated and take turns batting the balloon over the net. The balloon can be batted as often as necessary. When one side fails to control the balloon and allows it to touch the floor, the opposition scores. The scoring team serves. The players rotate so that everyone has a chance to be positioned near the net and also in the rear. The game ends after a designated point total is reached.

Variation

Place a small marble inside the balloon, which adds unpredictability to the game.

Battlefield

Equipment

* several small nerf balls

* masking tape

* two padded rulers

Set-Up

Mark the boundaries with masking tape. Place a strip of masking tape halfway across the center of the play area to establish the centerline. Divide the group into two equal teams. The teams space themselves and sit on opposite sides of the centerline, facing each other. Each team selects a doctor. Give both doctors a syringe (padded ruler) and each team several balls.

Directions

On the signal to begin, the players attempt to hit the opposition with the balls and immobilize them. If a player is hit with a ball on the fly, he or she lies on the battlefield and is frozen. Each team's doctor can give a shot to a frozen player by touching him with the syringe in order to revive him. The goal is to hit the opposing team's doctor, because doctors cannot give themselves shots and nobody else can become the doctor. The first team to hit all of the opposing team's players wins.

Variation

If a player catches a ball that has been thrown at him or her, the player who threw the ball is inmobilized.

Break the Code

Equipment

* sheets of assorted colored paper

Set-Up

Prepare ahead of time a large quantity of 1" squares of colored paper. Unknown to the players, assign a point value to each color using both positive and negative numbers (e.g., white = 1 point, black = 2 points, red = -1 point, etc.). Divide the group into equal teams of five to six players seated at a table.

Directions

Everyone places their head on the their tables so that they cannot see while the colored squares are scattered around the room. Set a time limit. On the signal to begin, each team tries to collect as many valuable colored squares as possible. When the time limit expires, players return to their table, and their points are tallied and recorded. After a few rounds, the players may break the code and deduce which colored squares are positively valued and which ones are not, bypassing negatively valued colored squares for other teams to collect. The team that scores the most points after a predetermined number of rounds wins. The point value of each color is announced at the conclusion of the game.

Carpet Relay

Equipment

✳ carpet squares (two per team)

Set-Up

Divide the group into equal teams of four to five players. Define the start line and select a finish line across the room. Team members line up behind the start line. Give the first player in line on each team two carpet squares.

Directions

On the signal to begin, the first player on each team puts down a carpet square and steps on it, then turns around and retrieves the one behind him or her. He or she then places that carpet square in front, steps on it, and turns around and retrieves the carpet square from behind. This continues until the player reaches the finish line. Then the player puts the carpet square in the outstretched hand of the next player in line. The next player continues in the same manner. If a player steps off his or her carpet square, he or she must return to the start line. When a team successfully moves themselves from start to finish, they win.

Human Three-in-a-Row

Equipment

✳ nine chairs

Set-Up

Set up nine chairs in three rows of three. Divide the group into two equal teams. Team One stands on one side of the chairs and Team Two on the other. The players on each team number off so that there are the same number of students on each team.

Directions

To begin play, call out a number. The two players with that number (one from each team) rush to sit down in any two chairs as quickly as possible. After they are seated, call out another number. The game continues in the same manner until three teammates from either team have successfully sat three-in-a-row either horizontally, vertically, or diagonally. If neither team sits three-in-a-row, a tie is declared. The players return to their team, and the game is played again.

Link Four

Equipment

 * assorted colored chalk

 * deck of playing cards

 * yardstick

Set-Up

Use a yardstick to draw a large grid on the chalkboard. Divide the group into equal teams of four to five players seated at a table. Label each team a different alphabetical letter and give them a differently-colored piece of chalk. Separate the playing cards by number and give each player on a team a differently-numbered card beginning with the number two, continuing consecutively until everyone has a card (i.e., each team has a player with a number two card, three card, four card, etc.). The remaining cards are discarded.

Directions

To begin play, call out a number. The player with that number (one from each team) rushes to the chalkboard and writes his or her alphabetical letter in an unoccupied square. The game continues in the same manner until a team links their alphabetical letter in four consecutive squares horizontally, vertically, or diagonally.

Variation

Prepare ahead of time questions about a variety of subjects. One at a time, ask each team a question. If a team answers the question correctly, they write their alphabetical letter in an unoccupied square.

Maze Craze

Equipment

* masking tape

* paper and pencil

Set-Up

Arrange strips of masking tape on the floor six rows long and three columns wide so that it resembles the diagram below. The players line up behind the start line. Draw the identical pattern on a sheet of paper. Secretly design a maze the players must follow.

Directions

To begin play, the first player in line steps on a strip of tape in the first row. If he or she steps on the correct strip of tape, he or she continues; if not, you say, "Buzz," and it is the next player's turn. Players may move horizontally, vertically, or diagonally but must step on at least one strip of tape in each row. The game continues in the same manner until a player successfully completes the maze without interruption.

Row 6	_____	_____	_____	
Row 5	_____	_____	_____	Masking Tape Strips
Row 4	_____	_____	_____	
Row 3	_____	_____	_____	
Row 2	_____	_____	_____	
Row 1	_____	_____	_____	

_____

Start Line

Quick Sketch

Equipment

* colored chalk

* slip of paper and pencil
  for each player

* two containers

* wastebasket

* watch or clock

Set-Up

Divide the group into two equal teams seated at tables. Give each player a slip of paper and pencil to write down one word. Then collect all the slips of paper and divide them evenly into two containers, one for each team. Place the containers at the foot of the chalkboard. The players on each team number off so that there are the same number of students on each team.

Directions

Set a time limit. On the signal to begin, the first player from each team rushes to the chalkboard and takes a slip of paper out of their team's container. The player reads it, throws it in the wastebasket, and then tries to draw the word. Their team tries to guess the word by looking at the drawing. When the word is guessed, the second player draws another slip of paper, and so on until all the words in the container are guessed or the time limit expires. If a player is unable to draw a picture of the word, that slip of paper remains in the wastebasket and he or she can take another. No letters or words are permissible, only pictures. The drawer may not speak until someone guesses correctly. The first team that finished all the words in their container without any passes or guesses the most words before the time limit expires wins.

Variation

Prepare ahead of time the words on strips of paper for both teams to draw.

Quick Spell

Equipment

✳ sheets of white paper

Set-Up

Prepare ahead of time a large quantity of 1" squares of white paper. Mark both sides of each square with a different letter of the alphabet. Include some squares with a "?" symbol to represent any letter. Divide the group into equal teams of five to six players seated at a table.

Directions

Everyone places their heads on their tables so that they cannot see while the white squares are scattered around the room. Set a time limit. On the signal to begin, each team tries to collect as many white squares as possible. When the time limit expires, the players return to their tables and arrange their letters into as many words as possible. Proper names and slang terms are not permissible, and the words must have at least three letters. Points are awarded for the number of letters in each word.

For Example:

✳ three-letter words = 1 point

✳ four-letter words = 2 points

✳ five-letter words = 3 points

The team that scores the most points after a predetermined number of rounds wins.

Variation

Each team that uses all their letters in a round receives 10 bonus points!

Touch-and-Go Memory

Equipment

✳ no equipment required

Set-Up

The players remain seated at tables.

Directions

Decide who will begin. Have that student leave his or her chair, touch an object in the room, then return to his or her seat. The second player chosen must touch the first object plus a new object. The third player must touch in sequence the two objects already touched plus a new object, and so on. The players are eliminated if they forget to touch an object, touch an object out of order, or talk during the game. The game continues in the same manner until one player remains.

All-Touch Kickball

Equipment

* ✳ playground ball

* ✳ four bases

Set-Up

Divide the group evenly into two teams. A baseball diamond or similar play area is needed for this game.

Directions

The fielding team stands behind the baseline, covering all the play area. The fielding team rolls the ball toward home base and waits for the kicker to kick the ball. After the ball is kicked, the kicker runs to each base without stopping. Kicking team players are scorekeepers and count one run for each base the kicker touches. When the ball is fielded, it must be thrown from one fielder to another. As soon as a player throws the ball, he or she sits down. When all the players are sitting down, the kicker stops running. If the ball is caught on the fly, no runs are scored. When all the players have kicked, the teams switch places. The team that scores the most runs wins.

34

Battle Ball

Equipment

* several jelly balls

Set-Up

Divide the group into two equal teams. A basketball court or similar play area is needed for this game. Each team occupies half of the court. Choose two goalies for each team. Goalies stand outside the opposite ends of the court. This puts each team in a crossfire between goalies and the opposing teams. Give each team several balls.

Directions

On the signal to begin, the players attempt to hit the opposition with the balls. The players become goalies if a ball strikes them below the shoulder level, the opposition catches their throw on the fly, or they drop the ball attempting to catch the ball on the fly. Once the ball bounces, it may be picked up and thrown at the other team. Original goalies replace the first and second team players hit. Only the goalies may retrieve balls outside the court on their side. When one team is eliminated, the other team wins.

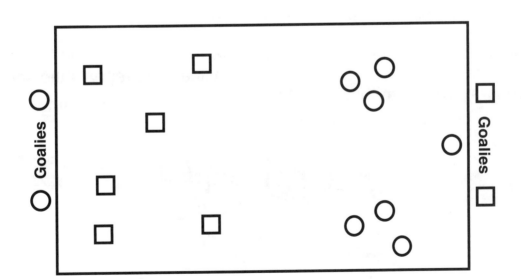

Bedlam

Equipment

* four traffic cones

Set-Up

Place a traffic cone in each corner of the play areas, forming a square. Divide the group into four equal teams. Each team forms a line behind a cone, facing the center.

Directions

To begin play, call out a specific direction that the players follow (i.e., diagonal, left, or right). On this command, each team attempts to walk as quickly as possible to the new corner. The first team to get all its players to the new corner wins that particular round. When the group grasps the idea, give several directions at once. There will be bedlam in the center as all four teams crisscross. The game continues in the same manner until a designated point total is reached.

Variations

1. Have players hop, skip, etc., instead of walk.

2. Have the first player from each team follow the directions and then tag the outstretched hand of the next player in line, who repeats the same procedure. The team that has all of its players back in its original corner wins.

Cageball Throw

Equipment

* beach ball

* several playground balls

* four traffic cones

Set-Up

Place a traffic cone in each corner of the play area to establish boundaries. The area in the middle is a no man's zone. Place the beach ball in the center of the no man's zone, equidistant from each line. Divide the group into two equal teams. Give each team several balls.

Directions

On the signal to begin, each team attempts to move the beach ball across the opponent's line by rolling or throwing the balls at it. The players may enter the no man's zone only to retrieve a ball but must return to their side before rolling or throwing the ball. No one may touch the beach ball with his or her hands or feet. The team that moves the beach ball across the opponent's line scores a point. Play continues in the same manner until a designated point total is reached.

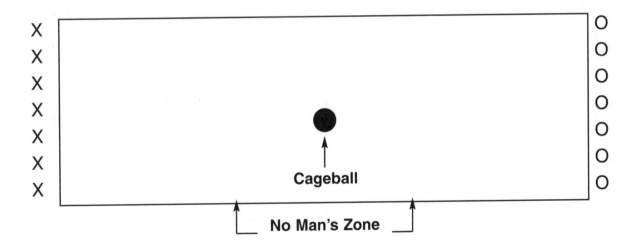

Capture the Flag

Equipment

✳ two flags

✳ several traffic cones

Set-Up

The play area needs to resemble the diagram below. Divide the group into two equal teams. Team One stands on one side of the field and Team Two on the other.

Directions

On the signal to begin, each team enters the other team's territory and attempts to capture the flag and then return to their own side without being tagged. Once players cross the centerline, they can be tagged and sent to jail across from each team's flag. If a player is in jail, a teammate can free him by getting to the jail without being tagged and then tagging him. Only the player being freed gets a free walk back to safety. The team that successfully captures the flag and runs it across the centerline wins.

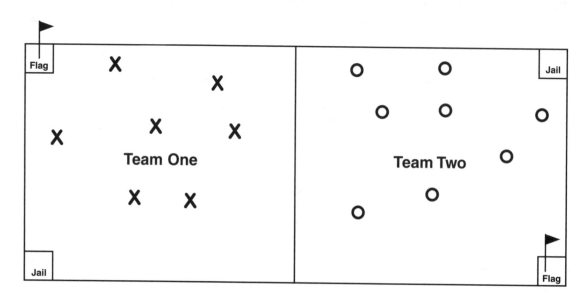

Circle Dodgeball

Equipment

* ✳ two jelly balls

* ✳ several traffic cones

Set-Up

The group forms a large circle. Place several traffic cones across the circle to establish the centerline. Divide the group into two equal teams. Each team occupies half of the circle. The players on each team number off so that there are the same numbers on each team. Place two balls a short distance apart on each side of the centerline.

Directions

To begin play, call out a number. The player with that number (one from each team) rushes to the inside of the circle, picks up his or her ball, and attempts to hit his or her opponent below the shoulder level. The remaining players forming the circle retrieve the balls on their halves of the circle and give it to their teammates inside the circle. When a player is hit, the opposition scores. The team that scores the most points wins.

Five Dollars

Equipment

* tennis racket

* tennis ball

* watch or clock

Set-Up

Choose a player to be the batter. The other players cover all of the play area or field.

Directions

Set a time limit. The batter uses the tennis racket to hit the ball to the other players. The players in the field try to catch the ball, either in the air or after it has bounced. Scoring is as follows:

* A ball caught on the fly (in the air) is worth $1.

* A ball fielded on the first bounce is worth 75¢.

* A ball fielded on the second bounce is worth 50¢.

* A ball fielded on the third bounce is worth 25¢.

The first player to earn five dollars or the player who has the most money when the time limit expires becomes the next batter.

Grab-Bag Relay

Equipment

 * slips of paper and pencil

 * two containers

 * wastebasket

Set-Up

Prepare on slips of paper ahead of time two sets of identical tasks to perform. Here are some sample tasks:

 * Balance a beanbag on your head and count to 10.

 * Dribble a ball with your hands five times.

 * Jump rope while counting to 10.

Evenly divide the slips of paper into two containers, one for each team. Define the start line. Place the containers an adequate distance from the start line. Divide the group into two equal teams forming two lines facing the containers.

Directions

On the signal to begin, the first player from each team rushes to his or her team's container and takes a slip of paper. The player reads it, throws it in the wastebasket, and then performs the specific task. Then that player runs back and tags the hand of the next person in line. It is now his or her turn to take a slip of paper and perform a task. The first team that performs all the tasks wins.

Roundabout

Equipment

✳ eight traffic cones

Set-Up

The play area needs to resemble the diagram to the right. Divide the group in four equal teams that are about even in speed. Each team forms a line behind the outside cone.

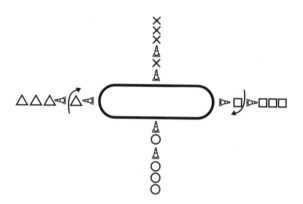

Directions

Set a time limit. On the signal to begin, the first players on each team run in a clockwise direction between the inside and outside cones and around the track, attempting to tag the runners of the other teams. Each player runs one lap before touching the outstretched hand of the next player in line, who continues the chase. When a player is tagged, he or she is out of the race and sits down in the middle of the track. The teams continue to run laps until there is either only one team remaining or for a designated period of time. When the time limit expires, the team that has the most players remaining wins.

Variations

Play the first game as described above. For the next game, have the players run in a counterclockwise direction. By doing this, the players who were being chased in the first game now have the opportunity to do the chasing.

Another variation would be to call out "Reverse" at certain points during the game. Players would then have to reverse their directions and begin chasing the players who were chasing them (and be chased by the players they were chasing).

Sizzleball

Equipment

 ✳ playground ball

 ✳ four bases

 ✳ four traffic cones

Set-Up

A baseball diamond or similar play area is needed for this game. Place the traffic cones in a square formation on the pitcher's mound. Divide the group evenly into two teams.

Directions

The fielding team stands behind the mound, covering all the play area. The pitcher or sizzler stands inside the cones. The sizzler rolls the ball towards  home base and waits for the kicker to kick the ball. After the ball is kicked, the kicker runs to third base, then second base, then first, and then home. The fielding team attempts to throw the ball to the sizzler before the kicker is standing on a base. The sizzler must catch the ball inside the cones. If the kicker is not standing on a base when the sizzler has the ball, he or she is out. If the ball is caught on the fly, the kicker is also out. More than one kicker may stand on a base at any time. However, only kickers who touch home base score a run. When all players have kicked, the teams switch places. The team that scores the most runs wins.

Squad Tag

Equipment

* stopwatch

* four traffic cones

* flag belts with flags (see **Variations**)

Set-Up

Place a traffic cone at each corner of the play area to establish boundaries. Divide the group evenly into two equal squads.

Directions

Decide which team will begin. On the signal to begin, one squad chases and attempts to tag the players of the other squad. When a player is tagged, he or she sits down. When all the players are tagged, the duration of time is recorded. Then the squads switch places. The squad that tags all the players of the other squad in the shortest amount of time wins.

Variations

Divide the group into several equal squads. Several squads at once chase and attempt to tag one designated squad.

Instead of having students tag each other, give all students flag belts with Velcro flags attached. When a player's flag is pulled off of his or her belt, that player is tagged out and sits down.

Three-Ball Kickball

Equipment

* ✳ three playground balls

* ✳ four bases

* ✳ basket

Set-Up

A baseball diamond or similar area is needed for this game. Place the basket near the pitcher's mound. Divide the group evenly into two teams.

Directions

The fielding team stands behind the mound, covering all the play area. The fielding team rolls the first ball towards home base and waits for the kicker to kick the ball. Immediately after the ball is kicked, the second ball is rolled. Immediately after the second ball is kicked, the third ball is rolled. After the third ball is kicked into play, the kicker begins to run to each base without stopping. Kicking-team players are scorekeepers and count one run for each base the kicker touches. The fielding team must field each ball and place each ball in the basket. When all the balls are placed in the basket, the kickers stop running. There are no foul balls. When all players have kicked, the teams switch places. The team that scores the most runs wins.

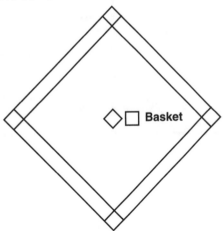

Tip the Cones

Equipment

✳ several playground balls

✳ eight traffic cones

Set-Up

Divide the group into two equal teams. A basketball court or similar play area is needed for this game. Each team occupies half of the court. Place four traffic cones at each end of the court. Give each team several balls.

Directions

On the signal to begin, players attempt to tip the cones of the opposition by rolling or throwing balls at them. Players may only use their feet to deflect the ball. The team that tips all of the cones first wins.

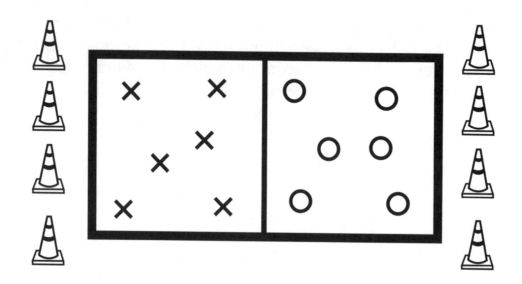

Touchdown

Equipment

* small object

* four traffic cones

* watch or clock (to keep time)

Set-Up

Place a traffic cone at each corner of the play area to establish boundaries. Divide the group into two equal teams. Each team stands at opposite ends of the play area. Decide ahead of time how long each quarter of play will be.

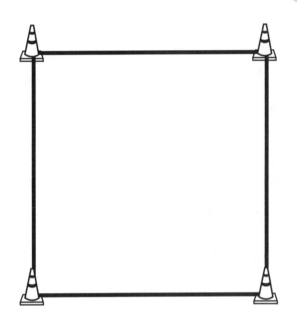

Directions

Decide which team will begin. One team huddles, where one player is secretly given an object to hide in his or her hands. The other players are decoys and they also clasp their hands as if they have the object. The other team forms a line on their goal line. On the signal "Hike!" the team possessing the object runs towards the opponent's goal line. Meanwhile, the other team attempts to chase and tag as many players as possible. When a player is tagged, he or she must stop immediately and show both hands to indicate whether or not he or she has the object. If the player carrying the object is tagged in the play area, play is stopped and the object is given to the opposing team. It would then be their turn to try to score. If the player who has the object crosses the opponent's goal line, he or she yells "Touchdown!" and his or her team gets six points. The winning team, of course, is the team that scores the most points in four quarters.

Alphabetical Index to Games